Fire and Water: Hawaiian Archipelago

Gene Allen Groner

To the Worldwide

Community of Christ Church

Other Books and eBooks by Gene Allen Groner

Journey of a Disciple

The Garden of Eden

Native American Prayers Poems and Legends

Native American Horses

Native American Fine Art

Micah's Fine Art

Fine Art by Sassan Filsoof

Son of the Most High

These Three Remain

The Helper: a Discourse on the Holy Spirit

Hallowed Be Thy Name

Deborah: Prophetess and Warrior

Saint Teresa of Calcutta

From Shepherd to King: the Story of David

The Nature of Angels

Speak To This People: Bible Prophets

For Such a Time as This: the Story of Esther

Prayers and Poems of Christ

In the Beginning

Introduction

I have always felt drawn to the Hawaiian Islands. As a young boy, I drew maps of Hawaii surrounded by the blue Pacific Ocean, dreaming of the day when I could go there and see all the beauty of this island paradise.

You can understand then, how delighted I was to receive as my first Marine Corps assignment the Marine Corps Air Base at Kaneohe Bay, Hawaii. I didn't even mind the uncomfortable and lengthy voyage over there on the crowded USS Eisenhower troop carrier from San Francisco, California.

Being there for two years was worth the wait and the long ship ride. I finally made it to the place I had dreamed about as a young boy, and I wasn't disappointed.

In this book about the Hawaiian Islands, I have included some personal stories, and some pictures of the places I have been. I think you will enjoy reading it and want to share it with a friend.

Chapter One

Fire and Water

Several atolls, numerous islets and surmounts, plus eight larger islands make up the island group known as the Hawaiian Archipelago.

This island group was first called The Sandwich Islands by Captain James Cook in 1798. He named them in honor of the 4th Earl of Sandwich, Admiral John Montagu of England. Since the 1840s the islands have been called Hawaii, named after the largest island in the chain.

2,500 miles from the mainland of the United States, Hawaii is nonetheless a state in the USA—the 50th state. The island chain itself is some 1,500 miles in length, with a total land area of 6,423.4 square miles.

The smallest islands are not inhabited and are known as the Northwestern Hawaiian Islands, or Hawaiian Leeward Islands (leeward meaning the side sheltered away from the wind).

These smaller islands include Nihoa (Mokumana) which is called Bird Island. Tallest of the ten uninhabited islands and atolls, Nihoa is the closest to the eight larger inhabited islands. The word Nihoa means "tooth" in the native language. Its name is derived from its jagged shape, which includes two main peaks. Nihoa's area is about 171 acres and it is surrounded by a large coral reef measuring 142,000 acres. There were Native Hawaiians

who lived on Nihoa a thousand years ago, according to prehistoric evidence, but little is known about them today.

In 1909 President Theodore Roosevelt set up a large area that included Nihoa as a federal wildlife reservation, and the area became part of the Hawaiian Islands Reservation. It later became part of the Northwestern Hawaiian Islands Wildlife Refuge and is now listed on the National Register of Historic Places.

Another of the smaller islands is called Necker Island (Hawaiian: Mokumanamana) meaning "branched island" or "island refuge," and is important for its prehistoric archeological contents of the Native Hawaiian culture. Necker Island is also part of the Northwestern Hawaiian Islands Wildlife Refuge.

View from top of Mokumanamana

With only a little more than 45 acres, the island is rocky with steep sides. The height of its tallest mount is 277 feet. Named after Jacques Necker, a finance minister of Louis XVI, there are few signs that anyone ever lived there for long. However, those who did come to Necker Island may have used this island as a ceremonial or religious site. 33 shrines have been found on island, and the legends from nearby islands point to Necker as a refuge for a race of small inhabitants (dwarfs) known as the Menehune who were chased from Kauai by larger and more powerful Polynesians.

These mythological dwarfs were said to be excellent craftsmen who inhabited forests and small valleys away from other people. They supposedly built roads, houses, temples, and fish bonds with great skill. They like to eat fish and bananas, and are said to have lived in the Hawaiian Islands before the first Polynesians.

Chapter Two

My Life at Kaneohe Bay on the Island of Oahu

I arrived at Kaneohe Bay, Hawaii in October of
1962. As a young enlisted man in the Marines,
I was assigned to live in one of the many
military barracks. The barracks were made of
concrete and steel and I lived on the second
floor with 20 other men. The first floor had a
large recreation room with pool tables and ping
pong tables, and a lot of other tables for
playing cards, checkers, and chess.

Between our barracks and the next one was a
"lanai" walkway, covered like a porch or
veranda with open sides for fresh air and a
clear view of the surrounding military base.

Beds were a steel frame on the floor, with a
thin mattress which was okay. In the summer
months we slept with a mosquito net over the
bed for safety. I don't ever recall being bitten.

The Marine Corps Air Station at Kaneohe Bay was a great place for me to work. I was stationed there from 1962-1964 as a radio operator in one of the Marine Helicopter hangars, and worked from 8 to 5 in one of the communications huts.

Working the daytime shift gave me the opportunity to take night courses at the University of Hawaii in Honolulu. I bought a car for $100 and drove off the base and across the Pali Mountain into Honolulu, about a 30 minute drive from the base.

At the University of Hawaii I studied a basic freshman course of study—english literature, philosophy, psychology, math, and economics. In the two years I was there, I managed to earn 24 college hours of credit—roughly the equivalent of one year of college. It was fun and I enjoyed learning. Plus it gave me a nice diversion from the military base life.

The University of Hawaii at the Manoa Campus

I loved the weather in Hawaii—what's not to love, right? No snow or Ice, and a moderate temperature year-round of 70-80 degrees. It rains frequently, but only for a few minutes and then the sun comes out again. The exception is in the wintertime, when the rain is the equivalent of our snow—it's called "Hawaiian Snow."

Funny, though, after two years I kind of missed the change of seasons, even the snow back in Missouri.

I remember getting off the bus in Missouri after two years in Hawaii, and stepping into 24 inches of cold snow—be careful what you wish for!

Makiki Branch of the Community of Christ Church in Honolulu, Hawaii

During my two years in Hawaii, I attended the Community of Christ church in Honolulu, known as the Makiki Branch, named for the neighborhood where it was located. It was a good experience for me, and I enjoyed going to the denomination where I was a member.

There I met a lot of wonderful people. The Yasukawa family was especially kind and hospitable to me, inviting me to their home after church for lunch, and encouraging me to

sing in the church choir. I'm not a great singer, but I like to sing, and I really liked singing in the choir.

Rayette Yasukawa was an attractive girl who had a graduate degree in music from the University of Hawaii, and we took a liking to each other. We went on a number of dates, but that's as far as it went. She was really an accomplished pianist who earned a living by teaching piano. She tried to teach me one evening, but I just couldn't seem to pick it up.

I also dated a pretty Japanese girl for a while. Her name was Lisa Asama, and we sang together in an Episcopal choir at her church a few times.

I think that was the extent of my dating while stationed at the air base. But one of the things I did like to do was sailing in Kaneohe Bay at the air base. I was able to do that quite often.

My favorite place to eat out in Honolulu was the Greene Turtle. It was a restaurant and bar located on Kapiolani Boulevard near Waikiki Beach. I went there quite often with some of my friends from the Marine base.

They had a great piano player, and the patrons would sing along with the performers from the University of Hawaii music department—usually a different one each night. The singing was fantastic and lots of fun for everyone. We sang a lot of the songs from the hit musicals, like South Pacific, Music Man, Camelot and so forth. Great fun. The décor was interesting too. The ceiling was covered with beer mugs of every kind, from all over the world, hung up on cup hooks—it was really colorful and unique.

The Greene Turtle Sports Bar and Grille

I have so many good memories of my time in Hawaii. For example, across from Waikiki Beach was the International Marketplace, which featured nightly entertainment from local Hawaiian celebrities like Joe Kameamea, fire dancers, hula dancing in grass skirts, and an occasional luau. Most of the entertainment was free. Of course there were a lot of local specialty shops for the tourists to browse through. There were always plenty of tourists and servicemen and women—military personnel stationed at the Marine Corps Air Station, Pearl Harbor Naval Yard, Wheeler Air Force Base, and Schofield Barracks Army Base—all located on the island of Oahu—set up before and after World War II.

Today, Honolulu is completely different from how it was in 1962. My wife and I went there a number of years ago and couldn't believe our eyes. So many people and cars it was difficult to get a clean breath of air. In the evening we walked to the Ala Moana Shopping Center, where I bought her a nice ring to wear. As we stood there looking out toward Waikiki—which could no longer be seen from there—my eyes filled with tears. I was heart-broken to see all the concrete buildings, cars, and tourists. It was difficult to find a way through all of that just to get a glimpse of the ocean.

I remembered the many times I would go to the park at Waikiki, near where my wife and I

were standing that evening, and look out over the sandy beaches to the beautiful Pacific Ocean, clean and blue. The warm trade winds would gently blow across my face and hands—it was truly a Paradise on Earth.

But that was then. It is so different now. Now you must go to the other islands to see and feel such beauty.

I suspect you had better hurry, before they become just like Oahu. I pray that they don't.

Maui was great. We spent a week there one year, and it was still pristine and beautiful. We were in the very nice Intercontinental Hotel on the beach, compliments of my company. I went snorkeling and running up and down the beach, and enjoyed a luau dinner in the evening—with dancing and entertainment that was tremendous. There was a brunch on the veranda overlooking the sea that was out of a picture book.

The table was set with all kinds of food—delicious and lovely to look at. On one table there was a huge "horn of plenty" that was overflowing with all kinds of fresh island fruit. Everything there was the very best.

We really liked the village of Lahaina, an old whaling village with a 300 year old Banyan tree with several benches underneath the overhanging branches of the tree.

300 Year Old Banyan Tree at Lahaina on Maui

The village of Lahaina used to be called "Lele" meaning "relentless sun." It was once the capital of the Kingdom of Hawaii in the old days.

Now Lahaina is on the National Register of Historic Places, and it is the best place in the world to view Humpback Whales in the winter months.

Humpback Whale in Pacific Ocean in Maui HI

Full View of Humpback Whale at Maui, Hawaii

Lahaina is loaded with historic places, including old specialty shops, theatres, and great dining.

There are wonderful hiking trails and marvelous pristine beaches. This was one of the best trips my wife and I have ever taken, and we've been all over the world.

There's the Kona Coffee Festival on Maui, in addition to the Hawaii Food & Wine Festival and Kapalua Wine & Food Festival featuring world-class chefs and cuisine. There's even a Lahaina Pineapple Festival with fresh island pineapple to enjoy. Lots of great entertainment to suit every age and every taste. You'll love it!

So many things I've been privileged to do and see in Hawaii—no wonder that to me it is still Paradise on Earth.

In November of 1964 I returned to the mainland of the United States of America. I spent my 21st birthday in San Francisco, where I mustered out of the Marine Corps at Travis Air Force Base near San Francisco.

I thoroughly enjoyed my tour of service in the Marines, and it still comes up in my dream life from time to time. The only reason I didn't continue a military career was that I was committed to finishing my university education, which I did at Park University in Parkville, Missouri.

Graduating with honors in the Master of Arts Program in Psychology, I spent over 30 years as a Financial Advisor and Investment Counselor, a wonderful career that provided well for my family of five children and nine grandchildren. I have no regrets

My wife and I now live in Independence, Missouri, in the same town we settled in when we got married some 55 years ago. We have a lovely 2 story Colonial home on an acre of wooded land, where we enjoy working in our gardens and where I write all my books and articles. God has blessed us abundantly.

Historic Mackay Hall at Park University

Park University has been named in US News and World Report's Best Colleges and Universities in the USA.

It is a beautiful campus, and Mackay Hall at Park is listed on the National Registry of Historic Places in the USA.

I am the first person in my family to get a college degree, and I know my mother and father would be pleased. May they rest in peace.

Chapter Three

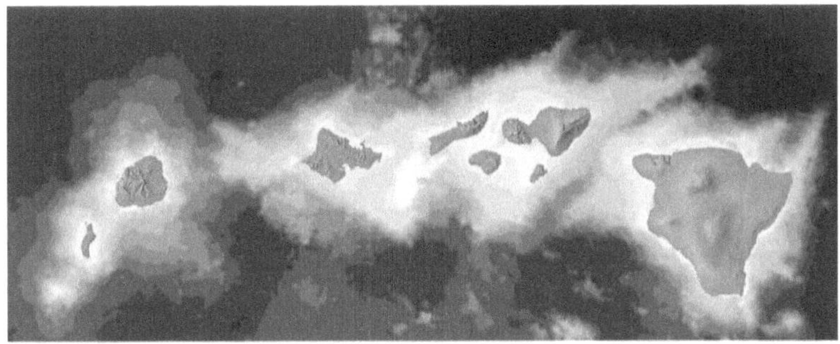

How Hawaii Was Formed

Now we come to the place where we discuss just how the Hawaiian Island Archipelago was created.

According to the National Oceanic Service, the chain of islands known as the Hawaiian Island Archipelago was formed by "hotspot volcanism," a term I had not heard before this book.

The Earth's outer crust is made up of a series of tectonic plates that move over the surface of the planet. In areas where the plates come together, sometimes volcanoes will form. Volcanoes can also form in the middle of a plate, where magma rises upward until it erupts on the seafloor, at what is called a "hot spot."

The Hawaiian Islands were formed by such a hot spot occurring in the middle of the Pacific Plate. While the hot spot itself is fixed, the plate is moving. So, as the plate moved over the hot spot, the string of islands that make up the Hawaiian Island chain were formed.

The Hawaiian Islands form an archipelago that extends over a vast area of the North Pacific Ocean. The archipelago is made up of 132

islands, atolls, reefs, shallow banks, shoals, and seamounts stretching over 1,500 miles from the island of Hawaii in the southeast to Kure Atoll in the northwest.

According to the National Geographic Society, the island of Hawaii formed 4.5 million years after Kauai. Kauai is the first of the Hawaiian Islands to be created. The big island of Hawaii is still forming through its current volcanic activity, as it is sitting on the hotspot miles beneath the Pacific Ocean.

Current Eruption of Volcano in Hawaii

Earth's rocky outer shell, its crust, is actually made of dozens of huge pieces of rock known as tectonic plates. These plates ride on currents of molten rock in the upper mantle, which lies just below the crust. Activity in the mantle and crustal plates results in earthquakes and volcanic eruptions. Most of these seismic events take place where two plates come together or tear apart.

The Hawaiian Islands, however, sit in the middle of the Pacific plate. They lie over a hot spot, where magma from the mantle pushes to the surface. The Hawaii hot spot remains in one place while the Pacific plate moves steadily northwest. Hawaii's "Big Island" is still being formed by Mauna Loa and Kilauea, two volcanoes currently sitting over the hot spot. Loihi, an undersea volcano, also sits above the hot spot and will likely become the next Hawaiian island.

Niihau, the most northwesterly of the main Hawaiian Islands, is about 6 million years old. Hawaii, the youngest of the main islands, remains close to the hot spot, and at less than 1 million years old, it is still forming as the hot spot feeds lava to its active Kilauea volcano.

Mauna Kea, one of six volcanoes that have formed the island of Hawaii, is the tallest mountain on Earth at 9,966 meters (32,696

feet, 6.2 miles). This is 1,116 meters (3,661 feet, 0.7 miles) taller than Mount Everest and roughly the same height in the atmosphere where commercial airplanes fly. With 4,205 meters (13,796 feet, 2.6 miles) above sea level, more than half of Mauna Kea's height falls below the surface of the ocean, with its base reaching 5,761 meters (18,900 feet, 3.6 miles) deep. Mauna Kea is dormant, having last erupted 4,600 years ago. Kohala is the island's oldest volcano and is now extinct. Hualalai last erupted in 1801, and Mauna Loa last erupted in 1984. Kilauea has been erupting actively since 1983.

The geologic landscape of Hawaii's islands has changed greatly over time, which has also impacted its ecologic landscape. As Hawaii's volcanic islands rise and fall, organisms must adapt to a series of transitional habitats both above and below the ocean surface. In terms of the habitats and species that are part of Mauna Kea—from its mountain peak to its ocean deep—the colossal mountain is not only tall, but high in biodiversity as well. Mauna Kea's variety of terrestrial habitats includes stone deserts, shrublands, alpine woodlands, and tropical forests. These varied habitats are home to several endemic species that are only

found on Hawaii or the Hawaiian archipelago. The ocean habitats that characterize Mauna Kea are equally varied and full of life. The greatest quantity of marine life is found between the surface and a depth of 1,189 meters (3,900 feet, 0.7 miles) in the sunlight zone and twilight realm. Below 3,900 feet are the midnight zone and abyss, which are dark, cold, under high pressures, and lacking in food. Species in these extreme environments have developed unique adaptations to regulate their temperatures, protect themselves, help them locate food, communicate, and find mates.

Fish Living in the Deepest Oceanic Waters

Chapter Four

Stories About Water

As I think about the waters of the Pacific Ocean, I am reminded of a personal testimony I wrote several months ago. Allow me to share the story with you now:

Living Water

"The water that I will give will become a well of water springing up to eternal life."

These are the words of Jesus that he spoke to the woman of Samaria that warm summer day. She was thirsty. He gave her water to drink. She was tired. He offered her rest for her soul. She was weary of the life she had lived. Jesus gave her a new beginning, and hope for a better life.

Now Jesus learned that the Pharisees had heard that he was gaining and baptizing more disciples than John—although in fact it was not Jesus who baptized, but his disciples. So he left Judea and went back once more to Galilee.

Now he had to go through Samaria. So he came to a town in Samaria called Sychar, near the plot of ground Jacob had given to his son Joseph. Jacob's well was there, and Jesus, tired as he was from the journey, sat down by the well. It was about noon.

When a Samaritan woman came to draw water, Jesus said to her, "Will you give me a

drink?" (His disciples had gone into the town to buy food.)

The Samaritan woman said to him, "You are a Jew and I am a Samaritan woman. How can you ask me for a drink?" (For Jews do not associate with Samaritans.)

Jesus answered her, "If you knew the gift of God and who it is that asks you for a drink, you would have asked him and he would have given you living water."

"Sir," the woman said, "you have nothing to draw with and the well is deep. Where can you get this living water? Are you greater than our father Jacob, who gave us the well and drank from it himself, as did also his sons and his livestock?"

Jesus answered, "Everyone who drinks this water will be thirsty again, but whoever drinks the water I give them will never thirst. Indeed, the water I give them will become in them a spring of water welling up to eternal life."

The woman said to him, "Sir, give me this water so that I won't get thirsty and have to keep coming here to draw water."

He told her, "Go, call your husband and come back."

"I have no husband," she replied.

Jesus said to her, "You are right when you say you have no husband. The fact is, you have

had five husbands, and the man you now have is not your husband. What you have just said is quite true."

"Sir," the woman said, "I can see that you are a prophet. Our ancestors worshiped on this mountain, but you Jews claim that the place where we must worship is in Jerusalem."

"Woman," Jesus replied, "believe me, a time is coming when you will worship the Father neither on this mountain nor in Jerusalem. You Samaritans worship what you do not know; we worship what we do know, for salvation is from the Jews. Yet a time is coming and has now come when the true worshipers will worship the Father in the Spirit and in truth, for they are the kind of worshipers the Father seeks. God is spirit, and his worshipers must worship in the Spirit and in truth."

The woman said, "I know that Messiah" (called Christ) "is coming. When he comes, he will explain everything to us."

Then Jesus declared, "I, the one speaking to you—I am he."

She had many husbands. Jesus told her she only needed one. He was the one she needed.

Jesus is the one we need.

Jesus and the Woman at the Well—John 4:1-42

Behind my house is a living spring. Every day it brings forth fresh water from the earth.

It never fails, never falters, it never forgets. Fresh water every day without missing a drop.

When I think of the water from our living spring, it reminds me of Jesus and his everlasting love, the kind of love I need. I am no different than the woman from Samaria.

We are the same, she and I. We both drink from the same well, the well touched by the hands of Jesus.

The same hands that healed the blind and the lame. The same hands that blessed the bread and the wine. The same hands that prayed to the Father. The same hands that blessed the little children; that lifted the fearful and drowning Peter up from the Sea. The same hands that raised Lazarus from the dead.

Hands that will never grow old or tired. Hands that are made for touching and holding and blessing.

Hands that are full of love for the poor. Hands reaching out to heal and to bless and to forgive.

How I love those hands. Those are the hands that I long to touch. Those are the hands that we all want to hold. Those are the hands that created the world. Those are the hands that heal the broken-hearted. One day those same hands will take us home. Home to the place where we belong.

Home to the place of light and love. Home to the place where the Father waits. Home to the place of living water.

That's my home. Heaven.

The following story is a story of faith. I think we can all identify with one or more of the characters in the story. See what you think:

Jesus Walks on the Water

Immediately Jesus made the disciples get into the boat and go on ahead of him to the other side, while he dismissed the crowd. After he had dismissed them, he went up on a mountainside by himself to pray. Later that night, he was there alone, and the boat was already a considerable distance from land, buffeted by the waves because the wind was against it.

Shortly before dawn Jesus went out to them, walking on the lake. When the disciples saw him walking on the lake, they were terrified. "It's a ghost," they said, and cried out in fear.

But Jesus immediately said to them: "Take courage! It is I. Don't be afraid."

"Lord, if it's you," Peter replied, "tell me to come to you on the water."

"Come," he said.

Then Peter got down out of the boat, walked on the water and came toward Jesus. But when he saw the wind, he was afraid and, beginning to sink, cried out, "Lord, save me!"

Immediately Jesus reached out his hand and caught him. "You of little faith," he said, "why did you doubt?"

And when they climbed into the boat, the wind died down. Then those who were in the boat worshiped him, saying, "Truly you are the Son of God."

I am a lot like Peter. I get all fired up and ready to go, but when the going gets rough, fear starts to take over and I lose faith—I start to sink.

With Jesus it's not enough to get off to a fast start. He wants us to keep on going till the end. That's endurance and that takes real faith. The kind I want to have but don't always have. I want to do better.

Here's a story of mine about endurance:

Run and Not Grow Weary

Those who hope in the LORD will renew their strength. They will soar on wings like eagles; they will run and not grow weary, they will walk and not be faint (Isaiah 40:31, NIV).

There is no failure for the faithful. Real faith does not grow weary.

When I was running marathons, I never cared about winning a race. The most important thing to me, the thing I was faithful to, and the thing that kept me injury-free year after year, was finishing the race.

That's the only thing that motivated me to keep on running, long after my strength had left me, long past the time when I was exhausted, and long after my muscle's store of glycogen had been depleted.

I was focused on keeping my eye on the goal. The goal was always to finish the race. Remaining faithful to that goal has been the main motivating force of my life. Staying faithful and finishing the race.

Saint Paul the Apostle said it this way, in 2nd Timothy chapter 4, verse 7 (NIV): "I have fought the good fight, I have finished the race, I have kept the faith."

The marathon is a race that is 26.2 miles in length, named in honor of Pheidippides, who was a Greek soldier and a messenger made famous for running from the Battle of Marathon to Athens in Greece. He completed the distance in order to announce to the officials in Athens that they had won the victory.

He, like Paul, finished the race and kept the faith. That was his task. To go the distance and announce the victory. To this task he was faithful to the very end.

Being faithful to God and family has been the motivating force in my life. When I was baptized at the age of eight, I promised to follow Jesus and be faithful to God throughout my entire life. When I married my wife 55 years ago, I promised to remain faithful to her for my entire life, no exceptions.

I grew up without a father. It was difficult for me at times, but my mother was the one who really made the sacrifice for us three boys. It wasn't easy for her. I love and respect her for all she meant to me, may she rest in peace.

My mother was the one who taught me to be faithful to family and to God. I took her message and example to heart long ago, and I still do.

Since I didn't have a father figure to show me how to be a good father, I learned from my father-in-law Orrice, who was always called "Bud."

I remember the memorial service in Stewartsville, Missouri for my father-in-law Orrice McCord. He was a man of God and a faithful family man. Those were the two most important things in his life, and the things that motivated him throughout his 91 years.

There were many friends and family who spoke at the memorial service, and at the close of the service, the pastor said these words from Matthew 25:21 (KJV), "Well done, thou good and faithful servant: thou hast been faithful over a few things, I will make thee ruler over many things: enter thou into the joy of thy Lord."

Everyone was silent. Everyone had tears in their eyes. I could never begin to match the love and devotion to God and family of that great man, Orrice McCord. He was indeed a faithful servant of our Lord Jesus Christ and a

man of great integrity. I think of him each and every day.

I look up to him as my real and spiritual father and mentor. He visits me often in my dreams. I know he is watching over me. May he rest in peace.

The last and final race of my life is the one I am running now. There are not many miles left for me to run. My goal is to finish the race, and hopefully to have those words spoken at my memorial service,

"Well done, thou good and faithful servant...enter thou into the joy of thy Lord."

Chapter Five

The Native Polynesian People of Hawaii

The Native Hawaiians or Aboriginal Polynesian people are called kanaka oiwi, kanaka maoli and Hawaii maoli in the Hawaiian language. There are currently about 527,000 who say they are Native Hawaiians (156,000 of them say they are purely Native Hawaiian, without any other racial mixture).

It is uncertain just when the Aboriginal Polynesian people first arrived in the islands, but it has been estimated to be somewhere in the third century. There are legends stating that they came from the Marquesas, Tahiti, or Samoa. No one is certain.

The Hawaiian language is known as Olelo Hawaii, but most Hawaiians today speak only English, the only language taught in the schools, with the exception of a few Hawaiian Language Immersion Schools.

Most of the primary and secondary schools in the islands are public, but there are a few private schools such as Punahoe, where Lisa Asama attended. Her Japanese family was well-to-do and could afford the private school.

There are two official languages in Hawaii, English and Olelo Hawaii.

Hawaii is known as the Aloha State. The Hawaiian word aloha means peace and harmony, kindness and compassion, and is used as both a greeting and when leaving.

Before leaving, I would like to conclude this book on the Hawaiian Islands with another personal testimony.

When I was in Hawaii, I was involved in a car accident. The car was totaled and I could have been killed. But God had other plans for my life—he intervened and saved my life.

God sent an angel to help me. Instead of the county morgue, I ended up in Queen's Hospital in Honolulu. The angel saved my life that day.

Let me tell you the story, I Believe in Angels.

"For he shall give his angels charge over thee, to keep thee in all thy ways" -Psalm 91:11

Ever since I was eight years old and in the third grade, I have believed in angels.

Riding my bicycle home from the grocery store one Saturday morning, I was struck by a car and knocked into the ditch. The car didn't stop to check on me. A little ruffled but otherwise unharmed, I brushed myself off and rode safely home. Mother met me at the door and could easily see my dirty shirt. Showing no surprise she asked, "Are you alright?" When I told her what had happened and she could see that I was okay she said, "I knew you would be safe because I prayed to God that he would send his angels to protect you." From that moment on I knew that angels were real, even if I couldn't see them.

More recently, in 2017 I was involved in a car wreck and woke up in a hospital. I barely remember the accident but will never forget how I was saved by an angel. The accident occurred in the country. For miles around there was no one but me. I hit a guard rail and totaled the car. I later learned that a young woman named Rachel found me and took me to the hospital. I never saw her, never heard her voice. But I knew without a doubt that God had sent an angel to rescue me.

God has always revealed himself through the ministry of angels. In chapter six of the Book of Daniel, God sent an angel to close the jaws

of the lions after Daniel was thrown into the lions' den. And we all know about the angel Gabriel's announcement to Mary, "The Holy Ghost shall come upon thee, and the power of the Highest shall overshadow thee: therefore that holy thing which shall be born of thee shall be called the Son of God" (Luke 1:35).

In her book, The Hiding Place, Corrie ten Boom tells of her remarkable experience in the Nazi concentration camp at Ravensbruck. Upon arrival, she and her sister Betsie, along with all the other women prisoners were told to remove all their clothes and put them in a pile. They were then handed their prison dress. Guards then searched the women before taking them to their barracks. Corrie had a Bible hidden in her clothing, along with some woolen underwear for her sister. Those items made a bulge in her dress and could easily be detected by the guards who searched the women again before taking them to their barracks. Before the final search, Corrie ten Boom prayed, "Lord, cause now thine angels to surround me, and let them not be transparent today, for the guards must not see me." The woman in front of her had hidden a woolen vest under her dress. It was taken from her.

The guards let Corrie pass, for they did not see her. Betsie right behind her was searched.

Miracles happen today like they did in the Old Testament and the New Testament times. Angels continue to minister in our lives today, as they have throughout all of history. They watch over us and protect us, and they guide us always toward our Father in Heaven. We may not see or hear them, but they are real and they are all around us. I believe in angels.

The Bible reminds us to "Be not forgetful to entertain strangers: for thereby some have entertained angels unawares" (Hebrews 13:2).

Thank you for letting me share.

Aloha!

Biography

Gene Allen Groner is a Christian writer and the author of more than 40 books and numerous articles on faith and spirituality. He lives in Independence, Missouri with his wife of 55 years, a retired public health nurse. His interests include reading and writing, gardening, and volunteer work in the community. He is listed in Who's Who in Missouri, and is a lifetime member of the National Honor Society in Psychology, Psi Chi.

Gene earned both the Bachelor and Master's Degrees with honors from Park University in Parkville, Missouri. He also attended the University of Hawaii and Saint Paul School of Theology. He and his family are lifetime members of the Colonial Hills congregation in Blue Springs, Missouri.

https://www.amazon.com/Gene-Allen-Groner/e/B077YTVSJZ

email: geneallengroner@gmail.com

Notes

Notes

www.ingramcontent.com/pod-product-compliance
Lightning Source LLC
Chambersburg PA
CBHW030358280726
48655CB00019B/2322